AF605730

ENGINEERING MARVELS OF AUSTRALIA

Australia's Bridges

Alison Hideki

Redback Publishing
PO Box 357 Frenchs Forest NSW 2086
Australia

www.redbackpublishing.com.au
orders@redbackpublishing.com.au

978-1-925630-77-0

Author: Alison Hideki
Editor: Michael Anderson
Proofing: Marianne Lindsell
Designer: Redback Publishing

Original illustrations © Redback Publishing 2018
Originated by Redback Publishing

Printed and bound in Malaysia

Acknowledgements
Abbreviations: l—left, r—right, b—bottom, t—top, c—centre, m—middle
We would like to thank the following for permission to reproduce photographs: (Images © shutterstock) p22t - Public Art installation in the Westgate Memorial Park, Bill Strong via Flickr, p22b - Westgate Bridge, p22t - Vicroads split, p23b - Westgate Bridge all reproduced from Public Records Office of Victoria

Every effort has been made to contact copyright holders of any material reproduced in this book. Any omissions will be rectified in subsequent printings if notice is given to the publisher.

A catalogue record for this book is available from the National Library of Australia

Contents

Bridge Structures

Australia's major bridges stand as marvels of engineering design and construction. They provide important links in road and rail systems, crossing rivers and estuaries, gorges, and ravines. Australia's major bridges have been built using different design and construction techniques.

HOLDING UP THE DECK

A bridge consists of three main parts: a bridge deck to carry the road or rail traffic, supporting structures to hold it up, and foundations for the supporting structures. The most common design consists of a deck supported from beneath by piers resting on foundations. The deck itself is built on huge beams, also called girders that span the distances between the piers. Hobart's Tasman Bridge and the Hindmarsh Bridge in South Australia are constructed in this way.

TRUSS SUPPORT

A truss supports a bridge deck. It is a framework of steel (or timber) that is as strong as a solid girder of the same dimension, but is much lighter. Brisbane's Story Bridge consists of giant trusses. The arch of the Sydney Harbour Bridge is one giant, curved steel truss.

PRE-STRESSED CONCRETE SUPPORT

If girders are made of concrete, they are strengthened with pre-stressed steel cables inside them. Pre-stressed concrete girders support Hobart's Tasman Bridge and South Australia's Hindmarsh Bridge.

Cantilever Structure

Huge bridge girders, too long and heavy to be lifted into place in one piece, are built in sections. The girder is built out from its supporting pier or abutment by the cantilever method. Each section is lifted and bolted to the extending girder above. The cantilevered girder is capable of supporting its own weight, and is balanced by a girder built from the same pier in the opposite direction. The huge trusses of Brisbane's Story Bridge and the box girders of Melbourne's Westgate Bridge were constructed using this method.

Story Bridge

Hindmarsh Bridge

cantilever

Westgate Bridge

Suspension Bridges

Suspension bridges use cables for support, but in a different way from cable-stayed bridges. The cables are slung between towers at the end of the bridge, and the bridge deck is hung from the cables. None of Australia's major bridges are suspension bridges.

Technology Time Machine! Computer Aided Design

Computers now play an important role in bridge design. CAD (Computer Aided Design) software packages assess such things as the soil and rock conditions of the bridges site, the expected traffic load, the materials to be used, the strength of the foundations needed, and the way the bridge will look. They also perform the complex mathematical calculations involved in the design.

BOX GIRDER SUPPORT

Some girders are hollow on the inside. They are called box girders. They have the same strength as a solid girder of the same size, but are much lighter. The deck of Melbourne's Westgate Bridge is supported by girders.

CABLE-STAYED BRIDGES

The decks of some bridges are supported by cables that are anchored to the top of high towers standing above the bridges piers. This method of supporting the long girders of the bridge deck is called cable-staying. The central spans of Melbourne's Westgate Bridge are cable-stayed. The entire deck of Sydney's Anzac Bridge is supported by cables, making it Australia's longest cable-stayed bridge.

THE STEEL-ARCH STRUCTURE

A single arched truss, such as the Sydney Harbour Bridge, can support bridge decks. On arched bridges, the deck is suspended or hung from the arch, and the ends of the arch are anchored on foundations at each end. These foundations are called abutments.

PIER NUMBERING

Bridge piers are each given a number. This aids communication between engineers and builders during construction and maintenance after the bridge is completed.

Sydney Harbour Bridge

The huge steel arch of the Sydney Harbour Bridge is recognised around the world as a symbol of Australia. It doesn't have the longest steel arch bridge deck in the world, but its arch is the highest.

The first European settlers in New South Wales knew that a bridge to cross the Harbour would be needed one day. Convict architect Francis Greenway first suggested it in 1815. In the years before the present bridge was built, Sydneysiders had only one way of crossing the Harbour - by ferry. The journey by road to the northern shore was 20 kilometres.

PROGRESS TOWARDS A SUITABLE BRIDGE

In 1890, the New South Wales Government established a Royal Commission to look at issues of transport in Sydney. It found out that the ferry traffic across the Harbour was getting heavier. But the ferry service couldn't be expected to cope as Sydney's population grew and spread further across the northern shores of the Harbour. A bridge was needed. In 1900, the New South Wales Government invited engineers worldwide to submit designs for a bridge to cross the Harbour in the city of Sydney. The designs submitted were considered unsuitable.

In 1916, the New South Wales Public Works Department, led by engineer JJC Bradfield, submitted a general plan for a bridge that would cross from Dawes Point to McMahons Point. Bradfield's plan was for a cantilever structure bridge with no supporting piers in the waters of the Harbour.

The Engineer

Engineer JJC Bradfield is known as the father of Sydney Harbour Bridge. The bridge road is called the Bradford Highway in his honour. At just 2.4 kilometres long, it is the shortest highway in Australia and perhaps the world. Bradfield also designed Brisbane's Story Bridge.

THE DESIGN CHALLENGE

- To build a bridge to span the Harbour near central Sydney.
- To span the Harbour without need of supporting piers in the harbour.
- To build a bridge with a deck high enough to allow ships to pass underneath.
- To build a bridge strong and wide enough to carry Sydney's traffic of trains, trams and vehicles, both motor and horse drawn.

Technology Time Machine! Just Girders and Cables

At the time of the building of the Sydney Harbour Bridge, steel in the form of girders and cables was the only material available to engineers for the support of bridge decks required to carry heavy loads across long spans, such as Sydney Harbour. Techniques for reinforcing concrete had not been developed at that time.

The Design

In 1922, New South Wales Public Works Department engineer JJC Bradfield was given the job of selecting a suitable builder for the new harbour bridge. Bradfield went on a worldwide search, and finally chose the English engineering company, Dorman, Long and Co of Middleborough. Bradfield worked tirelessly with the English company on the details of the final design for the bridge.

THE BUILDING CONTRACT

The contract required that:

- Either a single arch or cantilever structure be used.
- Only Australian workers be employed.
- The deck be wide enough to carry two railway tracks, two tram tracks and lanes for horse-drawn vehicles and motors cars.
- The deck is high enough above the water to allow ships to pass underneath.

THE DESIGN

The bridge would cross the Harbour from Dawes Point on the southern side to Milsons Point on the northern side.

A single steel-arch span would be used to hang the bridge deck from. This was cheaper than a cantilevered structure. It was also more rigid and more suitable for supporting the loads that the wide deck would have to carry.

The bridge deck would be hung on vertical poles called hangers descending from the arch. The arch would rest on and be anchored by huge, sunken concrete abutments on either side of the Harbour.

The design included four massive pylons, two at each end of the arch. They would serve no important structural purpose, but would make the bridge appear more solid. The south-eastern pylon would contain a lookout, 200 steps above the level of the deck.

STEEL, RIVETS AND GRANITE

Seventy-nine per cent of the steel used in the construction of the bridge was imported. Every one of the six million rivets used to construct the great structure was driven in by hand by workers using heavy sledgehammers. Granite for the pylons was quarried at Moruya, south of Sydney. A temporary town was built in Moruya to house the 250 stonemasons who dug it out of the ground.

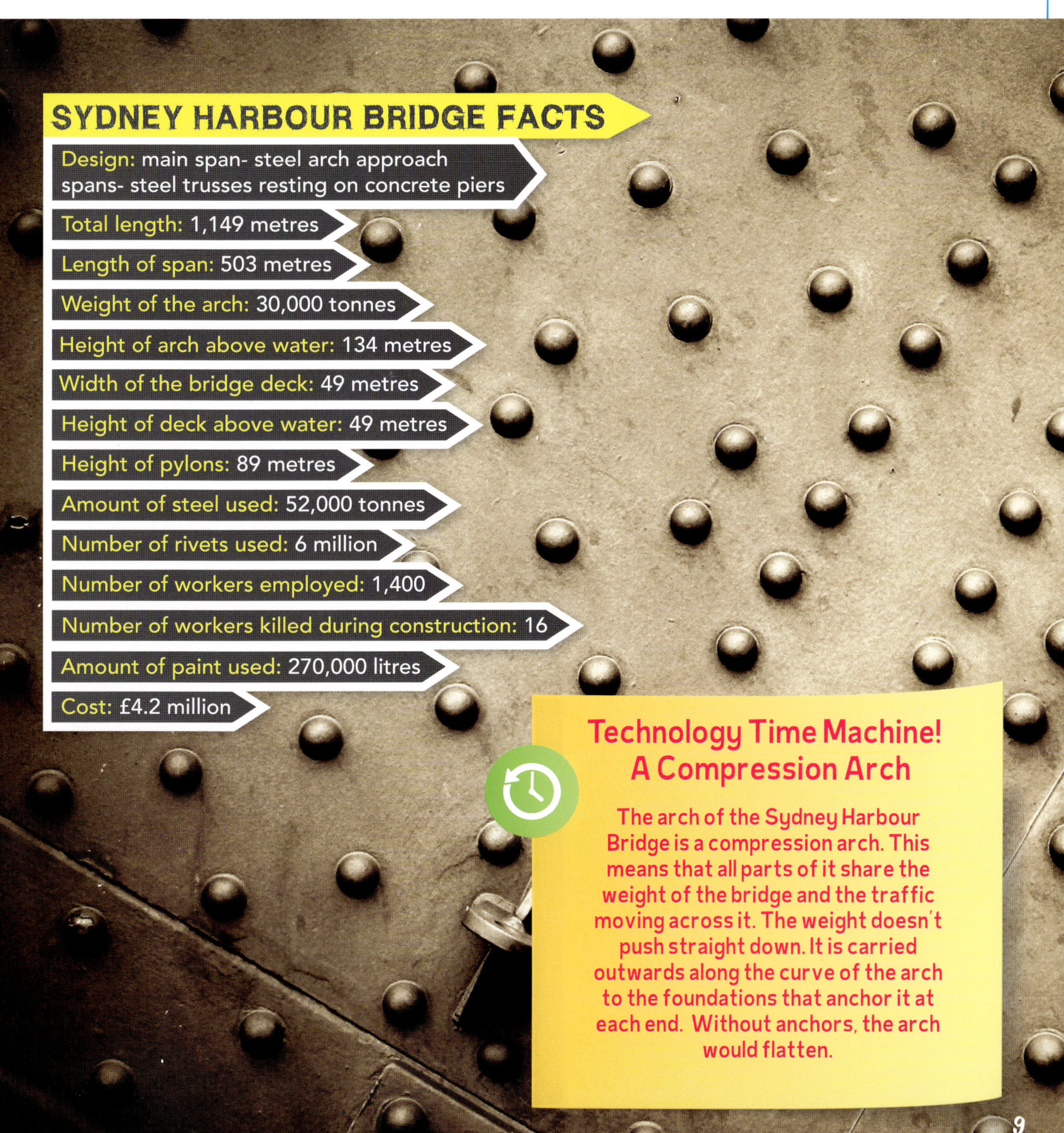

SYDNEY HARBOUR BRIDGE FACTS

- Design: main span- steel arch approach spans- steel trusses resting on concrete piers
- Total length: 1,149 metres
- Length of span: 503 metres
- Weight of the arch: 30,000 tonnes
- Height of arch above water: 134 metres
- Width of the bridge deck: 49 metres
- Height of deck above water: 49 metres
- Height of pylons: 89 metres
- Amount of steel used: 52,000 tonnes
- Number of rivets used: 6 million
- Number of workers employed: 1,400
- Number of workers killed during construction: 16
- Amount of paint used: 270,000 litres
- Cost: £4.2 million

Technology Time Machine! A Compression Arch

The arch of the Sydney Harbour Bridge is a compression arch. This means that all parts of it share the weight of the bridge and the traffic moving across it. The weight doesn't push straight down. It is carried outwards along the curve of the arch to the foundations that anchor it at each end. Without anchors, the arch would flatten.

Construction

Construction of the Sydney Harbour Bridge began on 28 July 1923. Before building began, workshops to fabricate the steel for the arch were built at Milson Point on the northern side of the Harbour. Work then proceeded in the five main stages.

THE ABUTMENTS

The huge concrete abutments to take the weight of the arch and to anchor it at each side of the Harbour were built. These consisted of huge concrete blocks set 12 metres deep into the rock.

APPROACH SPANS

The approach spans were built on steel trusses, which were supported by concrete piers. The piers were built on each side of the Harbour. Eight hundred houses in the path of the southern approach had to be demolished.

Dangerous Work

Building the bridge was dangerous work. Safety helmets were not compulsory for all workers. Scaffolds couldn't be built to protect workers on the bridge arch, and there were no safety harnesses that would tie them to the structure if they fell. Sixteen workers were killed during construction, seven of them while working on the arch structure.

Anchoring the Abutments

The abutments are the parts of the bridge that hold it down. So it is very important that the abutments are firmly secured in the ground. The Sydney Harbour Bridge abutments were anchored to the bedrock by cables 36 metres long. The cables were threaded through narrow tunnels bored through the rock and connected to each side of the abutments.

The Steam Engines Test

Before the bridge was opened to traffic, 96 steam engines were driven onto the bridge to assure the public that it was safe.

Opening Ceremony

The Sydney Harbour Bridge was officially opened on 19 March 1932 by New South Wales Premier JT Lang. The opening ceremony was interrupted when political protester Francis Edward De Groot rode onto the bridge and cut the opening ribbon. He was immediately arrested. The ribbon was replaced, and the ceremony proceeded.

THE ARCH

Work began on the arch in 1928. Two teams worked from opposite sides of the Harbour. Work on the southern half began a month before work on the northern half. This was to allow the engineers to learn from possible errors and avoid repeating them on the northern side.

The steel was transported across the Harbour from the workshops at Milsons Point on barges. Each piece was lifted into place by huge cranes fixed to the top of the growing arch. The cranes moved along the top of the arch as it grew. As the two sides slowly reached outwards and skywards from their abutments, they were supported by 128 cables anchored underground on the shorelines.

After two years, two sides of the arch met, and the cables supporting them were adjusted to bring them into exact line. They were riveted together on 19 August 1930. The cables were then removed. The single arch, stable and sturdy, was fixed in place.

THE DECK

Work on the deck began at the centre of the arch so that the creeper cranes, both now at the top, could move outwards and downwards to the shore. The cranes lifted the deck segments from barges below and suspended them on hangers attached to the arch. Construction of the deck took nine months.

THE PYLONS

The four pylons above the abutments were built from concrete and faced with granite blocks, quarried in Moruya, New South Wales. Two specially fitted-out ships transported the granite to the construction site.

The Bridge Today

Today, the Sydney Harbour Bridge carries eight lanes of motor traffic, two railway lines, a bike path and two steel-fenced walk paths, one on either side of the deck. The two original tramlines on the bridge were converted to traffic lanes when Sydney abolished its tram system in 1958.

TRAFFIC

When the bridge was opened in 1933, 11,000 vehicles crossed each day. In 1976, the one-billionth vehicle crossed the bridge. By 1980, 179,000 vehicles were crossing and the number was rising. The bridge was fast becoming unable to carry the number of vehicles crossing it without traffic jams. A second crossing was needed. A tunnel under the harbour just to the east of the bridge was built to solve the problem. It was completed in 1992, and now carries 75,000 vehicles per day. About 160,000 vehicles now cross the bridge each day.

A MAJOR TOURIST ATTRACTION

The Sydney Harbour Bridge is a major tourist attraction. Visitors come just to view it and marvel at its structure. Others climb the 200 steps of its south-eastern pylon to a viewing room and admire the spectacular views of the city, the Opera House and the Harbour.

TOLLS

Users of the bridge have always had to pay tolls. The money raised was used to repay the money used to build the bridge. The loan was finally paid off in 1988, but tolls have remained. They are now used to pay for maintenance. In 1933, the toll was six pence (five cents) for a car, and three pence for a horse. Today, drivers using the Harbour Bridge only pay tolls one way, on southbound journeys and the charge depends on the time of day. On weekdays the costs are:

6:30am - 9:30am	$4
9:30am - 4:00pm	$3
4:00pm - 7:00pm	$4
7:00pm - 6:30am	$2.50

BRIDGE CLIMB ADVENTURE

More adventurous visitors to the bridge can take the spectacular climb to the top of the arch. Each adventure lasts 3.5 hours and begins with a briefing session for safety. Climbers are supervised along the way as they climb steep ladders, walk across gantries and climb the rising curve of the arch at its edge. They are clipped to a safety rail by a harness, and are supervised along the way. The climb is not for people afraid of heights, and children must be at least 11 years old.

LIT UP BY FIREWORKS

The great arch of the Sydney Harbour Bridge is the centrepiece of spectacular fireworks displays in Sydney at occasions such as the new millennium in 2000, the Sydney Olympics in the same year, and New Year's Eve celebrations. Sydney's New Year's Eve fireworks on the harbour and the Harbour Bridge are well-known around the world.

MAINTENANCE

Maintenance work on the Sydney Harbour Bridge is continuous. Teams of painters work continually on the bridge, removing rust and painting the steel structure from top to bottom and end to end. A travelling platform suspended under the bridge deck enables workers to paint the deck's underside.

EXPANSION

Metal expands when it is heated and contracts when it cools. The top of the Sydney Harbour Bridge arch expands up to 18 centimetres due to changes in temperature. Two huge hinges at the base of each end of the arch allow for the expansion and contraction.

Story Bridge

The Story Bridge across the Brisbane River in Brisbane was built in the late 1930s. It wasn't built primarily to serve a traffic need in the city. It was constructed to provide employment for Brisbane workers, and to build the morale of Queenslanders during the distressing time of the Great Depression.

It is Australia's largest steel bridge designed and built entirely by Australians using only Australian materials. Almost all of the money spent in its construction was spent in Queensland to help boost the Queensland economy.

THE DESIGN CHALLENGE

The main design challenge was to provide foundations for the bridge abutments and approach piers on a solid rock foundation 40 metres below the thick sand layer that much of Brisbane is built on.

A steel cantilevered design was chosen. The structure consisted of two huge pointed-arch steel trusses, connected by a horizontal truss in the middle. The two arched trusses were to be cantilevered from the piers at each river's edge.

CONSTRUCTION

Construction began on 24 May 1935. It was completed in 1940, and the bridge was opened for traffic on 6 July.

The Story Bridge's approach spans, which rest on huge reinforced concrete piers, were built first. Massive excavations of sand were needed to reach bedrock for the foundations 40 metres below the surface. The steel truss central span was built in two sections, each reaching out from its supporting pier at the river's edge. Cranes on top of the trusses lifted the steel girders from barges on the river below to extend the trusses slowly across the river. Each truss was built out to a distance where it could support its own weight. The gap between them was then filled with a linking central truss section to make a continuous self-supporting truss. The bridge deck was built on the lower level of the truss.

Did You Know?

The bridge is repainted every seven years using 17,500 litres of paint.

THE BRIDGE TODAY

Like most inner city bridges in Australia, the Story Bridge is often choked with traffic jams at peak periods. The Queensland Government is planning to build a new inner city bridge to ease the pressure on the Story.

Today, the bridge has become a tourist attraction, offering visitors a bridge climb. The climb is one kilometre long across the top of the bridge structure, reaching a height of 80 metres. As well as 360-degree views of Brisbane, climbers can see out to Moreton Bay in the east and north to the spectacular Glasshouse Mountains.

Technology Time Machine! Through-truss Cage Design

The Story Bridge is a through-truss cage design. This means that the deck is built through the truss at its lower level and is encaged by the truss. In other truss bridges the deck is built on top of the trusses.

STORY BRIDGE FACTS

- **Design:** cantilevered steel truss
- **Length of the main span:** 281.6 metres
- **Total length, including approaches:** 1,375 metres
- **Width of deck:** 20.6 metres
- **Height of deck above river:** 30.4 metres
- **Concrete used:** 38,230 cubic metres
- **Steel used in structure:** 11,900 tonnes
- **Steel used in reinforced concrete:** 1,625 tonnes
- **Cost:** £1.5 million
- **Authority in charge:** Queensland Government
- **Chief engineer and designer:** JJC Bradfield, who also designed the Sydney Harbour Bridge
- **Builder:** Evan Deakin-Hornibrook

Tasman Bridge

Before Hobart's Tasman Bridge was built in 1964, Hobart residents crossed the River Derwent either by ferry, or on the floating Hobart Bridge. The Hobart Bridge was a curved, two-lane structure with one straight section that could be raised to allow ships and boats to pass through. However, by the late 1950s it was clear that a new bridge was needed. The suburbs on the eastern shore of the Derwent were growing, and faster access to these suburbs, and to the airport, was needed.

THE DESIGN CHALLENGE

- To span the River Derwent, which is just over one kilometre wide at the site of the bridge, is unevenly deep, and is heavily silted.
- To provide a deck for four lanes of traffic.
- To construct a deck high enough to allow ships to pass underneath.
- To provide spans wide enough at the deeper part of the river for ships to pass through.

CONSTRUCTION

Construction began officially in April 1960. Cofferdams were built first. These allowed areas of the river to be pumped dry so that the foundations for the piers could be built. Each foundation consisted of steel tubes filled with concrete. They were driven through the silt on the river floor to the bedrock below. Across the top of the steel tubes, concrete slabs were built for the piers to stand on.

The concrete piers were built next. Each pier consisted of two pillars. Each pillar was three metres wide and 0.75 meters thick. Each pair of pillars was joined at the top by a concrete crossbeam girder.

The concrete crossbeams of the bridge deck were lifted into place across the piers from barges on the river below by cranes standing on completed sections of the bridge. The deck was completed with the building of the road and side footpaths. Beneath the footpaths, water mains, electricity supply and communication cables were suspended. Construction was completed in December 1964.

TASMAN BRIDGE FACTS

- **Design:** pre-stressed concrete girder resting on concrete piers
- **Length, including approaches:** 1,430 metres
- **Length over water:** 1,077 metres
- **Height above the river at highest point:** 46 metres
- **Number of spans over the water:** 19
- **Number of piers supporting the spans:** 21
- **Number of piles forming the piers:** 216
- **Length of supporting beams:** 43 metres
- **Width of bridge deck:** 13.5 metres
- **Height of deck above water:** 46 metres
- **Amount of reinforcing steel used:** 5,283 tonnes
- **Amount of concrete used:** 74,000 cubic metres
- **Number of workers employed:** 400 at peak times of construction
- **Cost:** £7 million
- **Authority in charge:** The Public Works Department of Tasmania
- **Designing engineers:** G Maunsell and Partners, London, England
- **Builder:** Reed, Braithwaite, Stuart and Lipscombe, Salisbury, England

Technology Time Machine! Cofferdams

Engineers use cofferdams to build bridge piers in water. They are temporary structures used to dam water back from the site of the pier. Concrete box-like structures called caissons are sunk into the riverbed and then pumped dry to allow work on the riverbed.

Tasman Disaster

On 5 January 1972 at 9:27 pm, disaster struck the Tasman Bridge. The bulk carrier ship SS Lake Illawarra, carrying a full load of zinc, struck the base of one of the bridge piers. This caused two piers to collapse, bringing down 127 metres of bridge-decking above. Some of it crashed onto the ship and sank it. Seven crewmen died. Four of the many cars on the bridge plunged off the broken bridge to the River Derwent below. Five people died. Two cars managed to stop just at the edge of the break in the deck, teetering dangerously at the brink. Their occupants managed to escape and run back along the bridge warning other drivers of the danger ahead. A tourist bus approaching the gap managed to stop, turn and drive to safety. The bodies of the crewman and those who plunged into the river from above were never found.

THE CAUSE

On the night of disaster, SS Lake Illawarra was off course. It struck one of the piers (pier 19), well to the east of the shipping lanes. Had the ship struck the stronger, wider piers bordering the spans alongside the shipping channel, the bridge would not have collapsed. The Captain of SS Lake Illawarra was blamed for the accident.

An Eyewitness Account

A passenger on the tourist bus described the disaster:

"As we drove onto the bridge we saw a man rushing towards us, waving his arms. 'Just some nutter', the driver said over the bus PA. But then we noticed cars stopped ahead, some U-turning. We knew something was wrong. Then we heard from a driver that the bridge was down. Our driver started to turn, edging the long bus backwards and forwards around on the narrow bridge. We didn't think we would make it, we were all terrified it would come down. But it didn't, and we got off, and cheered the driver."

SS Lake Illawarra

REBUILDING

Rebuilding the Tasman Bridge began in October 1975. Before repair work began, a search was conducted to locate the exact position of the parts of the bridge and the ship on the river bed to ensure they didn't interfere with the construction. A fifth lane was added to the entire length of the bridge to cope with ever-increasing traffic crossing it. Work was completed in October 1979, at a cost of $44 million. During the reconstruction, ferry services across the river were increased and a temporary road bridge was built.

THE TASMAN TODAY

Today, the Tasman Bridge carries 65,000 vehicles per day across the River Derwent.

Westgate Bridge

The Westgate Bridge is Australia's longest bridge. It was built across the wide, lower part of the Yarra River to provide a road link between Melbourne's east and west. Until 1978, goods manufactured in the west had a slow journey through the densely populated western suburbs to Melbourne's ports for shipping. As early as 1929, a bridge across the lower Yarra River was suggested.

THE DESIGN CHALLENGE

- To build a bridge to rise from the flat, low lying land on either side high enough above the Yarra River to allow ships access to Australia's busiest port.
- To construct a deck wide enough to take the existing and expected future traffic entering the city from the west.

The Westgate Bridge combines two bridge structures. The approach spans are concrete box girders supported by huge concrete piers that rest on foundations reaching to the bedrock below the mudflats of the riverbanks. The longer central spans of the bridge are built from steel box girders. They are supported by huge cable-stays anchored on massive pylons that rise above the bridge deck.

CONSTRUCTION

Work commenced on the Westgate Bridge in 1970. The foundations for the 25 piers of the approach spans were built first. Steel-encased concrete piles almost two metres wide were sunk 62 metres below ground level. On them, the concrete piers were constructed.

The concrete box girders were raised in sections by huge jacks on the ground below, and bolted into position. The wider central sections that span the river were built out from each side and connected in the middle. The sections of steel box girder were raised by jacks on barges on the river. They were bolted in position. As the sections were built out to span the gap, they were given additional support by the steel cable-stays that were anchored to the pylons above the deck.

WESTGATE BRIDGE FACTS

- Design central spans: steel box girder with cable support
- Design approach spans: concrete box girder resting on concrete piers
- Number of central spans: 5
- Total length of central spans: 848 metres
- Total length: 2.6 kilometres
- Width of bridge deck: 35.6 metres
- Number of supporting piers: 26
- Number of traffic lanes: 8, plus 2 emergency lanes
- Traffic: motor vehicles only
- Height above Yarra River: 54 metres
- Total cost: $300 million
- Toll in 1978: 25 cents per vehicle, each way
- Authority in charge: Lower Yarra Crossing Authority
- Designer and builder: Freeman Fox, England

Technology Time Machine! Reinforced Concrete

Concrete is formed by mixing small stones called screenings, sand, cement, and water. The cement, which is made by burning lime and clay, binds the other ingredients. When concrete sets (cures) it is rock-hard. It has been used since the times of the ancient Egyptians and Romans. Today, concrete is reinforced by having steel framework embedded in it.

Collapse

Workers were concerned about safety from the early days of construction. A bridge using a similar box girder structure had collapsed in England, killing four workers. Chief engineer Jack Hindshaw assured the workers that safety precautions had been doubled. Hindshaw said that he himself would be spending six hours a day on the bridge, so he wasn't going to build one that could fall down.

DISASTER

At 11:50 am on 15 October 1970, the bridge span between piers 10 and 11, on the western side, collapsed. Thirty-five workers, some on the bridge itself, others underneath it, were killed. Chief engineer Jack Hindshaw was among the dead.

CAUSE OF THE COLLAPSE

When one section of the box girder structure was raised into position it didn't line up properly with its connecting section. Thirty bolts were removed from the connecting span to bring it into alignment. To save time, the bolts were not unscrewed to remove them. Instead they were tightened until they snapped. This caused the structure to groan, and the heat generated by stresses on the steel caused it to change colour, appearing to turn blue. Jack Hindshaw communicated with the engineers on the ground below. They ordered him to replace the bolts immediately. But there were no bolts on the bridge: new bolts had to be collected from below. Before they could be replaced, the span collapsed.

GOVERNMENT INQUIRY

A royal commission was conducted into the cause of the collapse. It concluded that neither the design of the bridge nor the materials used were at fault. The disaster was a result of mistakes made by the engineers in charge. Work recommenced on the bridge in 1971, and it was completed in 1978.

A LUCKY MAN

Paddy Hanaphy was the last man to leave the bridge before it collapsed. He was having lunch and sharing a joke with his workmates when he 'heard a rumble' looked up and saw his mates 'falling through the sky' from the collapsing bridge.

Technology Time Machine! Box Girders

Box girders are huge hollow beams. They are usually square or rectangular in cross-section, but they can be other shapes too. Box girders are made in sections, which are bolted or welded together. Both concrete and steel box girders were used in the construction of the Westgate Bridge. The box girders used on the approach spans of the Westgate Bridge are made of concrete reinforced with steel. Their hollow sections are trapezium-shaped. The upper sides of the girders are extended outwards on both sides. The extensions provide the support for the bridge deck, which is wider than the central part of the box girders.

The Westgate Today

Today, the Westgate Bridge is an important link in Melbourne's freeway system but it is barely coping with the increasing amount of traffic using it each day.

DEVELOPMENT IN THE WEST

The Westgate Bridge and its freeway links have made industrial and residential development to the west of Melbourne possible. The industrial areas have expanded, suburbs have grown, and new suburbs and housing developments have been built. This is due to the greatly reduced traffic times into the city that the bridge has made possible. Even some Geelong residents take this advantage and drive to work in Melbourne daily.

EVER-INCREASING TRAFFIC LOAD

The increased population and industries to the west of Melbourne made possible by Westgate Bridge, is now a problem for it. During peak times, lines of cars and heavy trucks slow to a crawl. An accident on the bridge can cause gridlock for hours.

In 2018, construction is expected to start on The West Gate Tunnel Project, which will provide a vital alternative to the Westgate Bridge. It is predicted to open to traffic in 2022.

BRIDGE MAINTENANCE

One million dollars is spent each year on bridge maintenance. One section of the road surface is repaired each year. The surface has to be removed and replaced. New tarmac can't be laid on top of old because it would add to the weight the bridge must support. Regular inspections of the box girders are carried out by maintenance engineers who have access to the insides of the box girders. In 2004, a complete safety review of the entire bridge was undertaken. Minor cracking in the steel of some of the box girders and some concrete piers was found. These have been repaired and the bridge is completely safe. In 2011, upgrades took place for two extra lanes.

Memorial Park

In 2004, a memorial park was built under the bridge near where the span collapsed in 1970. The park includes 35 sculptured stone monuments that commemorate each of the 35 workers killed by the collapse.

Hindmarsh Bridge

The Hindmarsh Bridge spans part of the Murray River to connect Hindmarsh Island with the town of Goolwa in South Australia. For 140 years before it was built, the only way to Hindmarsh Island from the mainland was to travel on a ferry from Goolwa, drawn by an underwater steel cable. The slow trip, and the size of the ferry, meant few people visited Hindmarsh Island.

DESIGN FEATURES

The bridge is built almost over the route of the old ferry to line up with the existing road approaches on each side. However, it was curved across the water so that the building of the pier foundations didn't interfere with the underwater cables that pulled the ferry across the river. This allowed the ferry to operate during construction.

The bridge structure curves upwards to its maximum height from the level of the riverbanks. This cut the cost of the project considerably, because the existing roads could be used to access the bridge at the riverbanks. No new elevated approaches were needed to lift the road to the bridge at the water's edge.

Nine piers support the bridge deck. This is more than are needed. Bridge engineers call this 'pier redundancy'. It means that should a vessel collide with and bring down a bridge pier, the bridge deck could not collapse.

THE DESIGN CHALLENGE

- To build a bridge at the site of the ferry crossing that would allow the ferry to operate during construction.
- To build, at minimum cost, a bridge that could withstand a collision with river traffic.

Sacred Sites

For 10 years the Hindmarsh Bridge plan was opposed by the Ngarrindjeri people because they believed it would disturb sacred Aboriginal sites. The matter was finally decided by a Royal Commission, which ruled that the bridge could be built.

CONSTRUCTION

Construction began in 1997 and was completed in 2001. Piles to support the bridge piers were built first. Hollow steel tubes were hammer-driven to the rock below the riverbed, and then filled with concrete. On these, platforms were built to support the bridge piers. Four parallel steel girders were laid across the piers along the length of the bridge to support the deck. The deck is made from reinforced concrete, 20 centimetres thick.

Time was saved in the construction by pouring the concrete deck as steel girders for each span were positioned. The timber formwork for the newly poured concrete was on a trolley riding on the steel girders. As each section of concrete set, the formwork was rolled to the next section ready for another concrete pour.

THE BRIDGE TODAY

The Hindmarsh Bridge has opened up Hindmarsh Island to tourist and residential development, and a huge marina has been built.

Technology Time Machine! Movable Formwork

Formwork is a timber frame, or box, to contain the concrete that forms the required shape of a concrete section of a building. Once the concrete has set (cured), it is removed. Formwork is built on the building site by carpenters. On the Hindmarsh Bridge project, the formwork for the concrete sections of the bridge deck was built on wheels so that it could be rolled onto the next girder without having to be dismantled and rebuilt for each concrete pour.

HINDMARSH BRIDGE FACTS

- **Design:** pre-stressed concrete girder resting on concrete piers
- **Total length:** 319 metres
- **Number of spans:** 10
- **Number of piers:** 9
- **Height above the Murray River at the highest point:** 14 metres
- **Total width:** 10.8 metres
- **Authority in charge:** Transport-South Australia
- **Designer:** Maunsell McIntyre
- **Builder:** Built Environs

Bridges Snapshot

RICHMOND BRIDGE (TASMANIA)

The Richmond Bridge, which crosses the Coal River 25 kilometres from Hobart, is Australia's oldest bridge. It was built in 1825 using convict labour. Built from sandstone, its four main arches rise from solid stone piers. Today Richmond Bridge is still open to traffic and is one of Tasmania's most popular tourist attractions, with an average of 200,000 visitors each year. In 2017, work took place on the bridge to help preserve it.

HAWKESBURY RIVER RAIL BRIDGE (NEW SOUTH WALES)

The Hawkesbury River Rail Bridge, which spans the Hawkesbury River at Brooklyn, New South Wales, was built in 1946. The bridge replaced one built in 1889. The stone abutments of the old bridge on the riverbanks at each end of the bridge were used in the new bridge. It consists of two parallel bridges. Each consists of seven arch-shaped steel trusses resting on concrete piers. The trusses support the decks that carry the rail lines linking Sydney with northern New South Wales towns and Brisbane.

NARROWS BRIDGE (PERTH)

The Narrows Bridge, crossing the Swan River at Perth, is two bridges. The first was built in 1959. The second matches it, and was built in 2001. Each carries four lanes of traffic, including a bus lane; the new bridge also has a bike lane. The Narrows Bridge links Perth with South Perth and forms an important part of the Kwinana Freeway. From 2007, a rail line linking Perth with its southern suburbs replaced the bus lanes across the bridge.

Four parallel concrete girders support each deck. They are supported by piers each consisting of four stout columns resting on foundations of concrete pads at river level. The bridge is only eight metres above water level.

Richmond Bridge

ANZAC BRIDGE (SYDNEY)

The Anzac Bridge links Darling Harbour with Sydney's western roads across Johnstons Bay. It is Australia's longest cable-stayed bridge. Two open, diamond- shaped concrete towers anchor the 128 cables that support the bridge deck, which passes through the middle of the towers at their widest point. It is 800 metres long and was built in 1996. The towers are 120 metres tall.

GATEWAY BRIDGE (BRISBANE)

The Gateway Bridge spans the Brisbane River east of the city to connect highways to Queensland's Gold Coast to the south and the Sunshine Coast to the north. Its structure is concrete box girder on concrete piers. It is 1.63 kilometres long with a central span of 260 metres. A duplicate bridge was constructed as part of the Gateway Upgrade Project, and completed in 2011, allowing for more traffic.

BOLTE BRIDGE (MELBOURNE)

The Bolte Bridge across the Yarra River was built in 1999. It is an important part of Melbourne's City Link traffic system. It is a concrete box girder structure with a central span of 490 metres. The two giant central towers of the bridge are 140 metres tall, and for appearance only.

MT HENRY BRIDGE (PERTH)

The Mt Henry Bridge is constructed from pre-stressed concrete box girders on concrete piers. It crosses the Canning River south of Perth and is an important link in the Kwinana Freeway. The bridge deck is a low level, graceful concrete structure resting on V-shaped concrete piers that stand at water level on concrete piles driven 20 metres in the riverbed below. The bridge has two lower side decks on each side for pedestrian and bike traffic. It was built in 1982 and is Western Australia's longest road bridge at 660 metres.

Bridges at a Glance

Gateway Bridge Brisbane
1986, concrete box girder on concrete piers 1.63km

Richmond Bridge Richmond, Tas
1825, stone arch 60m

Story Bridge Brisbane
1940, cantilevered steel truss 1,375 m

Hawkesbury River Rail Bridge Brooklyn, NSW
1947, steel trussed girder on concrete piers 240m

Narrows Bridge Perth
1982, pre-stressed concrete girders on concrete piers, 338m

Mt Henry Bridge Perth
1982, pre-stressed concrete box girder on concrete piers 660m

Hindmarsh Bridge Goolwa, SA
2001, pre-stressed concrete girders on concrete piers 319m

Tasman Bridge Hobart
1964, pre-stressed concrete girder on concrete piers, 1,077m

Westgate Bridge Melbourne
1978, concrete box girders and steel box girders, 2.6 km

Sydney Harbour Bridge, Sydney
1933, steel arch 1,149 m

Glossary

abutments constructed foundations at the land ends of a bridge

beam a length of steel, concrete or timber that supports a structure

box girder a girder consisting of three-dimensional framework of steel, concrete or timber bolted together

cantilever a horizontal structure attached to a vertical support

cofferdams temporary weirs used to hold back water at a building site

cubic metres a unit of measurement of volume: one metre high by one metre wide by one metre deep is one cubic metre

deck the part of a bridge that carries its traffic

formwork temporary timber work built to shape a concrete structure, such as a floor or beam

foundations structures that form the base on which the bridge or other structure is built

gantries a supporting structure, usually for equipment

girder a large beam

Great Depression a period in the 1930s of high unemployment that created poverty for a large number of people

morale the feeling of being in high or good spirits

piers structures that support a bridge deck from below

pile a column or pillar

pre-stressed concrete concrete that has been reinforced (strengthened) by having tightened steel cables placed inside it

rivets large steel bolts that are hammered into position

Royal Commission a government inquiry into an important matter conducted by a judge or group of judges

span a section of a bridge stretching between the supporting piers

steel arch arch made of steel trusses from which the deck of a bridge is hung

truss a girder made from a framework of steel, or timber, that is lighter than but as strong as a solid girder of the same size

Index

Find Out More

WEBSITES

Sydney Harbour Bridge
http://www.australia.gov.au/about-australia/australian-story/sydney-harbour-bridge

Tasman Bridge
https://think-tasmania.com/tasman-bridge/

Westgate Bridge Memorial
http://www.westgatebridge.org